ALLEN PHOTOGRAPHIC GUIDES

HO[illegible] CO[illegible]

CONTENTS

INTRODUCTION

The colour of a horse or pony is frequently the first thing the viewer observes and it can be important for future identification. Colour in any one animal can vary according to the season, the weather, the food it eats, its age and its general management.

The names of all horse and pony coat colours could be universally standardised if the idea of the four 'basic' colours, black, brown, bay and chestnut were adopted. These basic colours are the building blocks of all known colours and are made up of black or red pigment, or a mix of both. They may occur alone, or in any combination with the addition of dilute and white hairs anywhere on the animal's body. This results in the vast array of known coat colours. Any additions to the basic colours are inherited independently and are passed on to the offspring separately.

A worldwide adoption of simple colour definitions would ensure that studbooks become much more accurate and more valuable to researchers and breeders alike. Traditionally used names, which often mean different things to different people, need never disappear, but be included after the standardised names.

THE BASIC BUILDING BLOCKS: THE 'REFINED' COLOURS

BLACK

This is a uniform black. The head, trunk, legs, mane and tail are black, but may be jet black, ordinary black, or faded black, where the legs, mane and tail are slightly darker than the head and trunk.

BROWN

Almost black, but orange hairs appear on the muzzle, and variously behind the elbow, on the flanks, at the back of the hindquarters and sometimes around the eyes.

BAY

Bays appear in an enormous variety of shades, from dark mahogany to light sandy/orange red on the head and trunk, while the mane, tail and lower legs (the **points**) are black. In some bays, usually the paler bays, the lower legs, and sometimes the tail, exhibit paler hairs. Sometimes bays appear to be 'peppered with coal-dust', descending from the top of the body.

CHESTNUT

This colour is red based and ranges from very dark liver chestnut to light red-gold. The mane and/or tail may be darker, the same colour, or paler than the body.

AUTHOR'S TIP

Bays and chestnuts are frequently mixed up, especially where bays exhibit very little black hair and chestnuts seem to exhibit some black hairs. Bays have **black** rims to their ears and **black** ear tips, whereas chestnuts do not. Make a habit of examining the ear rims.

Jet black

Ordinary black, slightly faded

Brown

Dark bay

Red bay

Sandy bay

left Very dark liver chestnut

AUTHOR'S TIP

Always examine the coronet band and the pasterns. In true chestnuts, these are usually paler than the rest of the body.

AUTHOR'S TIP

To aid the correct description of the colour of a horse or pony, especially when additions to the basic colour are present, examine the head colour very carefully, not forgetting to examine the ear rims.

above Red chestnut

All the other horse and pony colours are built from these basic colours. They are, in effect, additions to the basic colours.

left Pale chestnut

THE DILUTE COLOURS

The dilute colours are composed mostly of three kinds of dilution, i.e. coat lightening. (The very rare 'champagnes' have been omitted deliberately.)

WILDCOLOUR

Both red and black pigment are considered to be diluted equally, though the mane, tail and lower legs are normally less affected than the trunk. The head is frequently a darker shade than the trunk. White hairs are not uncommon in the mane and tail, and on the lower legs.

Black wildcolour
Together with brown wildcolour, black wildcolour is also called blue, mouse or slate dun. The trunk is blue or brownish-grey but the head is darker. The points are mainly black.

Bay wildcolour Also called bay dun, or sometimes cream dun. This colour has a red/sand to cream trunk and a darker head. The points are mainly black. Sometimes the dorsal stripe is red instead of black.

Black wildcolour

Bay wildcolour

AUTHOR'S TIP

Wildcolours *always* have a darker **dorsal stripe**, while leg barring and shadows on the shoulders and neck are common; these are called **primitive** markings. These are the true **duns**. Bred together they should never produce a blue-eyed cream.

Chestnut wildcolour

Also called red dun, 'pink' dun, or cream dun. The colour is red/sand to cream on the trunk, with the head, points and primitive markings darker.

left Red chestnut wildcolour

below Cream chestnut wildcolour

left Red bay with black dorsal stripe and black ear rims

AUTHOR'S TIP

Do not overlook a dark dorsal stripe on the basic colours (*see left*); they are quite common.

Pangaré This is a primitive pattern, sometimes associated with 'wild-colour', that exhibits creamy hairs around the eyes, over the muzzle, behind the elbows, on the flanks and on the back of the quarters. It is seen on black, brown, bay and chestnut bases.

below and right
Dark brown pangaré

Bay pangaré

right Chestnut pangaré

SILVERDAPPLE

Silverdapple is thought to affect only black pigment but it is very variable in its effect and open to speculation. Since silverdapple has no apparent effect on red pigment, chestnuts are thought to carry it unnoticed. It is, in fact, uncommon to see obvious dapples on a silver-dapple, which makes one question the name. However, clipping the animal can sometimes make the paler dapples visible. The colour silverdapple is not recognised as existing in Britain, though it is not as uncommon as people imagine.

AUTHOR'S TIP

Be on the lookout for grey hairs in the mane and tail and on the back of the lower legs, especially in bays and browns. Also look out for any sign of black hairs on the ear rims and on the knees and hocks of 'chestnuts'. All these features may indicate the presence of the silverdapple dilution.

Black silverdapple Also called blue silver and may be confused with grey.

Brown silverdapple Also called chocolate silver and may be confused with liver chestnut.

Bay silverdapple Also called red silver and often confused with chestnut.

Black silverdapple foal, bay silverdapple mare

Chocolate silver

Light bay silverdapple

Bay silverdapple

Classically, extreme silverdappling of black is considered to produce a cream or mushroom-coloured animal with a pale mane and tail – with or without dapples. This colour is increasingly being noted in Britain today, and variously registered as 'cream' or 'chestnut'.

THE 'PALOMINO' DILUTES

This dilution mainly affects red pigment.

Black/black-brown single dilute The colour may be russet, or dark liver chestnut, but with black points. Sometimes the points are faded to a very dark liver chestnut.

Single dilute black/dark liver chestnut

Single dilute black/russet

AUTHOR'S TIP

The 'palomino' dilution is always visible in the winter coat, which is obviously paler than the basic colour. Mated together, these dilutes do not breed true. This dilution is stronger when inherited from both parents, producing the blue-eyed creams.

Bay single dilute Depending on the basic colour, this will vary from dark bay with a few pale highlights, to pale cream, all with black points. Dark dappling or smuttiness is not uncommon.

right Single dilute bay/sooty/dappled

Single dilute bay/golden buckskin

Single dilute bay/cream buckskin

Chestnut single dilute These range from smutty palomino, through golden palomino to dark-eyed, dark-skinned creams.

The double dilutes These are also called the blue-eyed creams. A bay base produces the perlino, while a chestnut base produces the cremello. Both have pink skin and pale translucent blue eyes but perlinos are usually a darker cream and have an even darker mane, tail and legs, while the mane and tail of cremellos are white.

top left Single dilute chestnut/smutty palomino

top right Single dilute chestnut/golden palomino

centre left Single dilute chestnut/dark-eyed, dark-skinned cream

centre right Double dilute bay/perlino

below right Double dilute chestnut/cremello

AUTHOR'S TIP

Any animal with a dark to pale gold body and black points, but with no dorsal stripe, is called **buckskin**. Some buckskins are true-breeding.

VARIATIONS ON A THEME OF WHITE

GREY

Grey is a progressive silvering with age. All greys will end up white. Grey is not a birth coat colour but appears in the second coat. A grey is usually born the colour it would have been had it not also carried the greying pattern.

The variations of grey are numerous as they gradually lighten but they may be described as **iron grey**, **mid-grey**, **dapple grey**, **rose grey**, **light grey** or **white**.

top Iron grey

centre Light grey, dark mane, tail and legs

below White grey

AUTHOR'S TIP

In the newborn foal, if the legs are darker than, or the same colour as, the body and one parent is grey, the foal will probably go grey. The birth coat colour should always be recorded.

If a dark skin gradually becomes pink, the animal has the **pinkie syndrome**. If there is a basic colour area anywhere on the body, the animal has a **blood mark**. The appearance of darker flecks that get denser with age indicates a **flea-bitten** grey.

right Rose grey

AUTHOR'S TIP

Grey is never an asset to colour breeding since it eventually destroys all colours and patterns. It is also associated with melanoma, a tumour caused by the accumulation of the pigment melanin.

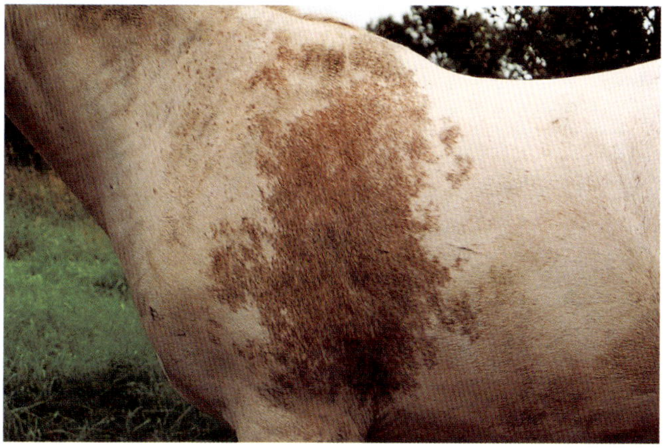

right and below Blood mark

ROAN

Like grey, true dominant roan is not a birth coat colour but, once it appears, though seasonably variable, unlike grey it remains the same throughout the life of the animal. The head and points retain the basic colour, while the trunk and upper legs exhibit a variable intermingling of white hairs.

Brown-black true dominant roan/blue roan

Black and dark brown true dominant roan This is also called blue roan. The points and the head are the basic colour, while the trunk and upper leg regions are variations of blue-grey to silver.

Bay true dominant roan Also called red roan. The colour characteristics are the same as the blue roan but the trunk and upper legs are reddish-grey varying from a dark to a pale red/gold tone.

Bay true dominant roan/red roan

Chestnut true dominant roan This is also called 'lilac' roan if liver chestnut is the basic colour, or called strawberry roan for any other variation of chestnut. The trunk and upper legs can be 'lilac', chestnut or 'pink' roan. The head and the points are the basic chestnut colour.

Many roans have white hairs in the mane and tail. Some animals are born with roaning. This can vary from light 'ticking' to extensively roaned areas, often associated with a lot of white on the head and legs. These are not true dominant roans.

AUTHOR'S TIP

Wildcolour and roan are often confused. The dorsal stripe is the key feature; wildcolours always have this stripe. Wildcolour and roan can occur together and when this happens the primitive markings are slightly roaned.

Liver chestnut true dominant roan/'lilac' roan

Chestnut true dominant roan/strawberry roan

Black tobiano/piebald

PIED

Pied means having a white patch, or white patches, on the body. All pieds have one thing in common – they can vary from almost totally dark to almost totally white and are called minimal pieds or extended pieds respectively.

Piebald means **black** with white patches, while **skewbald** means any other colour with white patches. Neither of these descriptions gives any idea of the **pattern** of white on the body.

For the best definition of pied markings the terms **tobiano** and **overo** are best applied. These definitions specify the *position* of body white markings. **Tovero** is a mix of tobiano and overo.

TOBIANO

Tobiano can be any colour with white patches if the white is dorsal in origin, i.e. the white runs down from the top (or back) of the animal. It looks as if white paint has been poured over the top of the body and runs down the sides to meet the high-level white of the leg. The head, chest and flanks are generally dark.

Black tobiano Also called piebald.

Brown tobiano Also called skewbald.

Bay tobiano Also called skewbald.

Chestnut tobiano Also called skewbald.

All previously listed colours in this book can be found in the tobiano pattern. **Tricolour** is a name unique to Britain and refers to an animal with white patches and any two other colours.

top Bay tobiano/skewbald

centre Chestnut tobiano/skewbald

below Grey tobiano/'blue' and white

AUTHOR'S TIP

Grey tobiano can cause problems in colour definition, not least because this description gives no idea of the basic colour. The colour of the young foal should be recorded. Often, grey tobiano is called **blue and white**. This may be a reasonable definition but **blue and white** can also be used to define black (blue) roan tobiano as well as black wildcolour (blue dun) tobiano, with or without the addition of grey. This situation makes studbooks valueless for researchers and breeders alike.

OVERO

Overos make up a large section of registered parti-coloured horse and ponies throughout the world, though in Britain very few overos are registered as being 'coloured'.

Unlike tobiano, overo can appear from solid-colour parents with no warning.

There are at least three basic patterns of overo but they all have the common feature of being ventral pieds. This means that the white originates not from the top of the animal, as in tobiano, but from below.

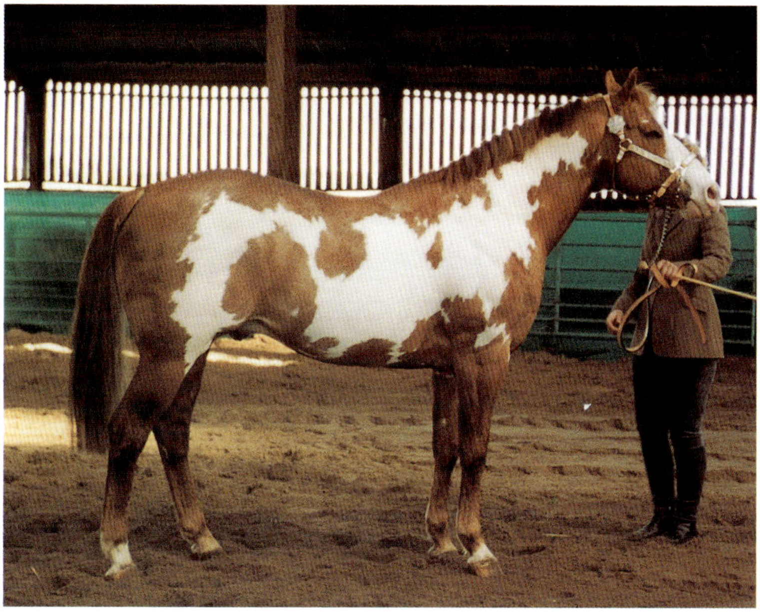

Chestnut frame overo

Frame overo This is a dark based horse or pony that appears to have white markings within a dark frame. The body gives the impression of having had white paint sprayed onto the sides of the neck, barrel, and quarters. The white edging is mostly broken-edged and the legs are mostly dark.

Chestnut splashed white overo

Splashed white overo This pattern looks like a negative image of the tobiano. The head, chest and flanks are white and the legs are mainly white. The tail usually has white in the lower reaches. The eyes are classically sky blue. Splashed whites look as if they have been lowered slowly, head down, into a deep pool of white paint. They are very rare parti-coloureds.

Chestnut sabino overo

Sabino overo This is the most common of all the ventral pieds and it occurs in numerous breeds and crosses. It can be incredibly variable. The pattern may be seen with or without the addition of a peculiar roaning. The common feature is the image that the animal has galloped through a shallow pool of white paint with its head lowered. There is usually high-level white on the legs, often up to or over the knees and the hocks, a white belly and white on the chest – which may even run up the front of the neck and join white that has extended back from the head. Some sabinos are extensively roaned or mottled and may be confused with spotted animals. The edges of all sabinos' white markings are usually broken or 'spotty'. The white on the head rarely extends over the whole of the cheeks. The eyes are often blue but a less vivid blue than the eyes of splashed whites. Very rarely, sabinos may be born white.

AUTHOR'S TIP

Where overos are obviously of mixed pattern origin, they should simply be described as overo.

The remarks in the tobiano section regarding the blue and white definition apply equally to overos.

Overos appear with many base colours, including black, brown, bay and chestnut, and, more rarely, any of the added patterns. However, chestnut overos are the most common. White head, leg and body markings are thought to be more extensive in chestnuts than with any other base colour.

WHITE-BORN

White-born is rather rare and may be the whitest extension of overo, tobiano, tovero and spotting. Sabino overo is the most likely pattern to beget white-borns. One cannot tell by looking at the animal what the pattern base is. The common features are the white hairs over virtually the entire body and pink skin. Some small areas of dark hair may be present, usually dorsally, for example, a dark forelock. Often some dark spots are visible on the skin and these may become larger with age. Some white-borns are viable but some die shortly after birth – the lethal white foal. The eye colour is never pink. The eyes may be blue, but more commonly they are dark. True **albino** has never been recorded in the horse. It is possible that a dominant white horse exists, but I doubt it.

White-born

Black leopard spotted

AUTHOR'S TIP

More than with any other colour or pattern in horses and ponies, it is recommended that spotted animals be photographed to aid identification. Spotted patterns are unique to every animal and often change during its lifetime. Photographs are also extremely useful for verifying the position of any white markings on the body, head and legs of other animals.

SPOTTED

Spotted patterns are variable but, unlike the pieds, the markings can change quite a lot during the life of an animal. Mottled skin, striped hooves and a humanoid eye are considered by some people to be essential in all true spotteds but they are not always present, particularly the humanoid eye.

I shall give only a very basic description of some spotted patterns. Virtually any colour can be found with white but darker colours are preferred. The addition of grey or dominant roan is disliked as it spoils the pattern.

Leopard spotting This is a white ground colour with spots of any size, shape or colour; the darker the spots the better the effect. Spotting usually extends over the whole body. Coloured patches are not considered to be part of the spotting effect.

The blanket Blanket markings are the most variable. They can appear with or without spots and with or without additional roaning. The spots may be large or small, and may be apparent only on the hindquarters, or extend forward over the ribs, either meeting a solid coloured area, or a roaned area. A blanket may be only a roaned area with no spots and this is the **frosted** pattern. Sometimes a dark dorsal stripe is visible together with a spotted blanket. Often the spots are raised so that a blind person could feel exactly where the spots are. A blanket-spotted pattern sometimes coats-out to become a leopard-spotted pattern.

Chestnut blanket spotted, appaloosa roaned, raised spots

Snowflake The snowflake pattern may also be called speckled. The animal often looks as if it has been out in a snowstorm. This pattern may not be evident in the foal coat but will appear later.

Chestnut blanket spotted foal

Marbled or varnished roan
This is a mix of white and coloured hairs but the areas over the body prominences are darker than the rest of the body. Peculiar white markings are often present on the lower legs. This pattern is rare in the newborn foal. It usually appears later in life, often when the foal coats-out.

Chestnut snowflake spotted

AUTHOR'S TIP

Appaloosa roan is not the same as any other roaning, though there may be some confusion. Also, the spotted patterns tend to be bilaterally symmetrical, unlike the patterns of parti-coloureds.

ADDITIONAL MARKINGS

Eye colour Equine eyes are usually really dark in colour. Sometimes, especially in the single 'palomino' dilutes, the eyes have a yellow hue. Perlinos and cremellos have pale translucent blue eyes. Splashed whites mostly have sky-blue eyes, while other animals, especially when white markings are near or around the eye, may have less vivid blue, or silver, eyes.

Yellow eye

Dark eye

Pale translucent blue eye

Dapples Be on the lookout for dappling on the body. Dapples are normally round, but in some greys they may be star shaped. Apart from on greys, dapples are most obvious on very shiny, dark summer coats, such as are seen in show horses and ponies.

The Prophet's Thumb Mark This is rare, and looks like a deep depression in a muscle area.

Prophet's Thumb Mark

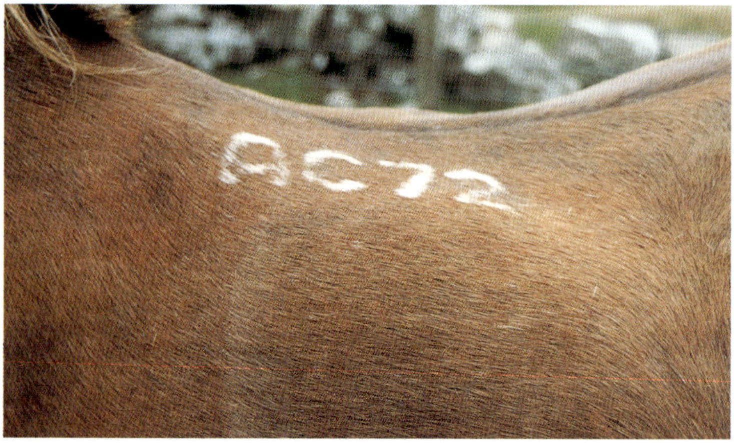

Freeze brand

Freeze brand This is a deliberately acquired marking for identification purposes. In greys the mark may just show the dark skin.

Fire brand This is another deliberately acquired marking for identification purposes but it is burnt into the skin with a hot iron. The coat colour in the brand area is usually darker in roans.

Be very observant and check for the presence of any **acquired marks** such as wire-cut scars and other cut scars, saddle or girth marks, etc. They are likely to be white. Also, be on the lookout for **ear tags, ear notches, hoof brands** and **tattoo marks**.

left Fire brand

Chestnuts Also known as 'night eyes'. These horny growths are to be found just above the knees in front, and just below the hocks behind. They are different on every animal and if drawn or photographed can be used to aid identification.

Whorls These are small areas where the hair flow meets as it changes direction. Their position and shape should be carefully noted, especially in animals with no white markings.

HEAD AND LEG MARKINGS

Head and leg markings are a very emotive subject. Just a browse through the photographs in this book will indicate just how difficult it is to define head and leg markings with absolute accuracy, which is essential for correct identification. Different names are too frequently given to similar markings and, likewise, the same name can mean different things to different people. This is a chaotic situation that must be avoided. White head and leg markings are very obvious on a clean horse or pony, especially in the summer coat, and they tend to alter very little, if at all, during the life of the animal. They can, therefore, be photographed, or drawn accurately.

The following are some simple and fairly universal definitions that may be used casually for white head markings.

Star Any white marking on the forehead.

Strip A white marking down the nasal bones.

Snip An isolated white marking between the nostrils.

Blaze A fairly wide white marking down the front of the face.

White muzzle White markings on both lips, usually including part of the nostrils.

Chin spot A white marking on the lower lip.

Leg markings vary in position and extent in the same way as head markings. It has been common in the past to make very loose definitions such as, white coronet, white heel, white pastern, white fetlock, white sock, white half sock, white stocking, white half stocking, etc., but nowadays these terms are best rejected in favour of more accuracy. For example, a white half stocking is much more accurately defined if described thus, 'having white to four inches below the knee on the left front leg, with an upside down 'v' on the front of the leg, and rising slightly at the back of the leg', and so on. This may sound complicated but it is accurate. Stripes on the hooves should be carefully defined.

Head markings should be similarly described for absolute accuracy.

ACKNOWLEDGEMENTS

The author wishes to thank her daughter, Deena Brooker, for taking the photographs of the chestnut wildcolour, the 'frame' overo and the Prophet's Thumb Mark. Thanks, also, to Christine Olmus for her photograph of her splashed white chestnut and to Wendy Campbell for the photograph of the author's chestnut sabino ponies. All photographs were taken at the request of the author.

British Library Cataloguing-in-Publication Data.
A catalogue record for this book is available from the British Library

ISBN 0.85131.764.2

Published in Great Britain in 2000 by
J. A. Allen an imprint of Robert Hale Ltd.,
Clerkenwell House, 45–47 Clerkenwell Green,
London EC1R 0HT

Design and Typesetting by Paul Saunders
Series editor Jane Lake
Colour processing by Tenon & Polert Colour Processing Ltd., Hong Kong
Printed in Hong Kong by Dah Hua International Printing Press Co. Ltd.